The Heyday of the Welsh Narrow Gauge

Peter Johnson

Ian ALLAN
Publishing

First published 1997

ISBN 0 7110 2511 8

© Ian Allan Ltd 1997

Published by Ian Allan Publishing

an imprint of Ian Allan Ltd, Terminal House, Station Approach, Shepperton, Surrey TW17 8AS. Printed by Ian Allan Printing Ltd, at its works at Runnymede, England.

Code: 9704/C3

Front cover: The former Penrhyn Quarry Hunslet *Linda,* running on the FR with a tender in 1962, passes Pen Cob, Boston Lodge. *Linda* is in Penrhyn livery with original sandpots but without the characteristic Penrhyn sand pots. *C.M. Whitehouse*

Back cover: The W&LLR first ran trains between Llanfair Caereinion and Castle Caereinion. On 7 April 1968 the Leicester Group of the Festiniog Railway Society made the W&LLR the destination of a coach trip. *J.B. Snell/C.M. Whitehouse Collection*

Right: Welsh narrow gauge steam at work in its natural environment: Dinorwic Quarry Hunslet 0-4-0ST *Michael* with a train of waste slate on Dyffryn level in September 1960. *Michael* was the last new steam locomotive built for Dinorwic Quarry, delivered in 1932. It went to Canada, along with stablemate *King of the Scarlets*, in 1965. *Geoff Lumb*

Title page: In 1956 the Welshpool & Llanfair was in its last year of British Railways operation as a goods-only line. Several 'last trips' were run for enthusiasts, the passengers riding in coal wagons, swept out for the occasion! Here we see a Stephenson Locomotive Society special crossing the road junction at Raven Square, Welshpool, at the end of the now-abandoned Town Section of the line, behind one of the W&L's pair of Beyer Peacock 0-6-0Ts. *C.M. Whitehouse Collection*

Introduction

The heyday of the Welsh narrow gauge railway would, for many, have been before World War 2, in the late 1920s and early 1930s. The Talyllyn had avoided the Grouping and was staggering along with its original stock; the Vale of Rheidol was being re-equipped by a benevolent Great Western, and although the GWR was not so generous towards the other narrow gauge lines in its empire, the Corris and the Welshpool & Llanfair, at least it didn't close them down. The Festiniog had also avoided the Grouping and was still operating its Victorian locomotives, including its unsurpassed Fairlies, and carriages, interspersed by its phenomenal gravity slate trains, while trying to come to terms with the infamous Col Stephens; the Snowdon Mountain loco fleet had been expanded and the Welsh Highland Railway and the Glyn Valley Tramway were still operating, albeit heading towards decline and closure.

Steam was king and there was little talk of closures or, heaven forfend, dieselisation. In the scenic splendour of North and Mid Wales narrow gauge steam railways were just right, for both passengers and goods. Unfortunately, Kodak didn't produce their first colour slide film until just before the war, so these railways were not photographed in their prime, as we would now like to see them, in colour. Therefore, for the purpose of this slim volume, the heyday of the Welsh narrow gauge was in the years after the war, in the 1950s and '60s.

Looking back over 30 or 40 years it is increasingly hard to imagine just what the Welsh narrow gauge railway scene was then like, for so much has since changed. There were, for example, no Llanberis or Bala Lake Railways in the north, nor the Brecon Mountain or Teifi Valley Railways in the south.

British Railways was still in the narrow gauge railway business though, carrying holidaymakers to Devil's Bridge on the Vale of Rheidol Railway out of Aberystwyth, and, even more extraordinarily, until 1956 carrying livestock to Welshpool market, and coal and coke back to Llanfair Caereinion, on the Welshpool & Llanfair Light Railway. Sadly British Railways' other flirtation with narrow gauge steam was all too brief, the Corris Railway being closed in 1948, after less than nine months in public ownership.

Elsewhere railway preservation had taken a hold. Firstly at Towyn, where the Talyllyn Railway was a remarkable survivor that required Herculean efforts to be made fit for continued operation and then (beyond the period covered by this book) extension to Nant Gwernol. Secondly, preservation took charge at Portmadoc, where the nine-years abandoned Festiniog Railway similarly called for an immense endeavour to recommence operation and to regain its inland terminus at Blaenau Ffestiniog.

At Llanberis, meanwhile, the Snowdon Mountain Railway was continuing to do what it had always done, ferrying tourists to Snowdon's peak. And on the coast, at Fairbourne, John Wilkins made great strides in rebuilding the Fairbourne Railway, which had almost vanished during its wartime closure.

The most notable feature of the postwar Welsh narrow gauge, however, and then only for those in the know, with the cheek or know-how to seek admission, were the steam-worked narrow gauge slate quarry railways, the homes of so many Hunslet 0-4-0STs, in all their variants collectively known as 'quarry Hunslets', and arguably the most attractive locomotives that the Leeds-based company produced. The quarries at Dinorwic and Penrhyn in particular are especially well regarded by the enthusiast for the Welsh narrow gauge railway, even those who, like this writer, were unaware of them until well after their railways had gone. They each had their own distinctive main lines

too, serving their respective ports on the Menai Strait; the Penrhyn line retaining the gauge of its quarries, while the Dinorwic line was the 4ft gauge Padarn Railway, also Hunslet-powered, conveying the slate in quarry-gauge wagons carried, in turn, on transporter wagons.

Regrettably, these quarries and their railways closed during the 1960s, just when they were becoming more widely known and photographed. The Padarn Railway went in 1961, followed by the Dinorwic quarry lines in 1967, while at Penrhyn the main line closed in 1962 and the internal lines the following year. Two miles of the Padarn Railway, from Gilfach Ddu, the Llanberis terminus, survive today as the Llanberis Lake Railway, although regauged to 1ft 11½in.

Tragically, the Padarn Railway's 4ft gauge Hunslets, unlike their famous predecessor, the 0-4-0 *Fire Queen*, escaped preservation, but the narrower-gauged locomotives did survive to be preserved, as far away as Canada and the USA, as well as in Wales and England. Indeed, of those newcomers to the Welsh narrow gauge scene, the Bala Lake, the Llanberis Lake and the Teifi Valley Railways operate only Penrhyn or Dinorwic locomotives, and the Brecon Mountain Railway started out running a quarry Hunslet from Pen-yr-Orsedd. In England the Launceston Steam Railway has become the largest centre of quarry Hunslets, with four, while others have made their mark on the Leighton Buzzard and West Lancs Railways, not forgetting those at the Bressingham and Hollycombe centres. One of the attractions of the quarry Hunslets in preservation must be their compact form, rendering them suitable for one-man restoration projects, such as the example presently being restored on the Isle of Man. In contrast, in the form of the extensively modified *Linda* and *Blanche*, the type has also had an impact on the Ffestiniog Railway.

While the quarry railways and their locomotives are here given pride of place, the passenger lines at that time were not without interest, largely due to their appearance, which

often seems unsophisticated to late 20th-century eyes. Due to the lack of resources, ie personal transport, for 'linesiding', most pictures taken during this period were of static subjects in stations; only with the introduction of faster film emulsions and cameras with higher shutter speeds did the photographing of moving subjects, even at speeds as high as 15mph, become commonplace.

Acknowledgements
As always, a book like this is a team effort, with each member indispensable. I extend my sincere thanks to Geoff Lumb, David Johnson (no relation) of Millbrook House, Roger West and Michael Whitehouse for so readily providing access to their collections. I also acknowledge the contribution made by Ian Allan's Peter Waller — the book was his idea. Handel Kardas became involved later on, and I am pleased to acknowledge his participation. Clearly it is not possible to provide chapter and verse in a book such as this — for further information the reader should refer to the various works of James I.C. Boyd published by the Oakwood Press and V.J. Bradley's indispensable *Industrial Locomotives of North Wales* published by the Industrial Railway Society.

Peter Johnson,
Leicester, November 1996

Note — Welsh names
While it is normal now for place and other names in Wales to be given the correct Welsh spelling, this was not always so in the period covered by this book. Railway and place names are therefore here given the spelling that was current at the time. For instance, 'Festiniog Railway' for pre–1970 references, 'Ffestiniog Railway' for more contemporary use.

The Quarries

Dinorwic

Above: The 4ft gauge Padarn Railway, opened in 1843, was built to replace an earlier 2ft gauge line. It ran for just over six miles from Gilfach Ddu at Llanberis, the present terminal of the Llanberis Lake Railway, to Pen Scoins, above Port Dinorwic on the Menai Strait. Traffic was at first horse-drawn, steam taking over in 1848. Padarn Railway Hunslet 0-6-0T *Dinorwic* is seen with a train of two loaded host wagons at Gilfach Ddu in 1953. The right-hand host wagon is sprung, to provide additional comfort for the brakesman riding in the caboose, and braked; one of these

vehicles is on display at the Narrow Gauge Railway Museum, Tywyn. *Dinorwic* is shown with a locally provided 'draught excluder' fixed in the cab opening. *P.B. Whitehouse/C.M. Whitehouse Collection*

Right: A train of empties returning to Gilfach Ddu, near Pen-y-Llyn, in September 1960. Before the Hunslets were obtained, two Horlock 0-4-0s, built in 1848, were used, of which *Fire Queen* survives at Penrhyn Castle. Sadly, an appeal to save one of the Hunslets failed to gain sufficient support to prevent them being scrapped in 1963. *Geoff Lumb*

Above: The Padarn Railway's *Dinorwic* was the first of its type to be delivered, in 1882, and the last to remain in service; it hauled the demolition trains when the line was dismantled, before being cut up in August 1963. The location is Gilfach Ddu in 1953. *P.B. Whitehouse/C.M. Whitehouse Collection*

Above: Amalthea was the second Padarn Railway Hunslet, new in 1886. Towards the end of their lives the original 'Midland Red' livery was changed for black, as seen here on 24 August 1961. *Ken Cooper/C.M. Whitehouse Collection*

Left: Setting the scene in Dinorwic. In 1953 one of the small Hunslets is surrounded by wagons, their double-flanged wheels being clearly visible on those on the right. The loads of those in the centre are being chained down in preparation for passage down one of the quarry's many inclines. The slate in the left-hand wagon also looks as though it is going for dressing, despite being loaded into a wagon often used for waste. These quarry lines, and those at the port, were of the unusual 1ft 10¾in gauge, a feature shared with the Penrhyn system. *P.B. Whitehouse/C.M. Whitehouse Collection*

Above: Holy War, a member of the 'Alice' class, was new in 1902. It was the last North Wales quarry steam locomotive in service when withdrawn in November 1967; three years later it was transferred to what is now the Quainton Railway Centre. Fitted with a cab and sprung buffers, it has been at the Bala Lake Railway since 1975. *Holy War* was photographed on the Penrhydd Bach level on 27 August 1964. *Roger West*

Left: Also freshly painted is *Maid Marian*, owned by the *Maid Marian* Locomotive Fund since 1966 and photographed at Gilfach Ddu on 28 March 1967, after it had been overhauled for its new owners. It was new in 1903 and has been based at the Bala Lake Railway since 1975. It spent six years at Bressingham and then moved to the Llanberis Lake Railway, where a cab was fitted, before moving to Llanuwchllyn. *Ken Cooper/C.M. Whitehouse Collection*

Left: Fresh out of the workshops and with a paint scheme which befits its name is *King of the Scarlets*, seen at Gilfach Ddu on 9 June 1965. Supplied to the quarry in 1889, it had been withdrawn after being damaged by a rockfall in 1962. The photograph shows the loco as prepared for export to Canada a few days later. *Ken Cooper/C.M. Whitehouse Collection*

Right: Seen on 28 August 1961 on Sinc Fawr, *Dolbadarn* was built in 1922 and was bought for the Llanberis Lake Railway at the quarry auction in 1969; it had been out of use for two years. Now fitted with a cab, *Dolbadarn* participated in the Ffestiniog Railway's 'Hunslet Hundred' gala, commemorating the centenary of *Linda* and *Blanche*, in May 1993. *Ken Cooper/C.M. Whitehouse Collection*

Above: In preservation since 1969, *Velinheli* has remained cableless and is now based on the Launceston Steam Railway in Cornwall. The brass dome was part of the saddle tank, this particular boiler actually being domeless. Built in 1886, *Velinheli* was recorded as being photographed on 19 September 1963. *Velinheli* also visited the Ffestiniog Railway in May 1993. *Ken Cooper/C.M. Whitehouse Collection*

Right: Wild Aster is seen with a train of slate waste in September 1960. The lack of activity and personnel in so many of these photographs is probably due to their being taken at break times. Built in 1904, *Wild Aster* has also found a new life on the Llanberis Lake Railway, where it is now known as *Thomas Bach. Geoff Lumb*

Penrhyn

Above: The Penrhyn Quarry main line was designed by Charles Easton Spooner, the Festiniog Railway engineer, and was completed in 1879, replacing a previous route. The railway was closed in 1962. *Blanche*, built by Hunslet in 1893, stands at Port Penrhyn on 14 September 1960. The bucket attached to the smokebox door handle was a feature of the Penrhyn Quarry Railway — it contained sand to supplement that in the tank–mounted sandpots seen either side of the chimney. *Roger West*

Right: Blanche waits to leave Coed-y-Parc with loaded slate wagons in September 1960. Since being sold to the Festiniog Railway in 1963, *Blanche* has been considerably modified, most noticeably by the addition of a pony truck and a tender cab and conversion to oil firing. *Geoff Lumb*

Left: Blanche again, caught *en route* from the back of a loaded train. *Roger West*

Right: In the 1950s and '60s the Penrhyn's Coed-y-Parc workshops became well known among enthusiasts for the disused locomotives stored there, some under cover but mostly outside; almost a narrow gauge equivalent of the later, and much better known, Barry scrapyard. Representative of this collection is Kerr, Stewart *Sgt Murphy*, photographed in September 1960. *Sgt Murphy* was the first of several second-hand locomotives obtained for the Penrhyn Quarries in the 1920s and '30s. In 1993 it was returned to steam by Winson Engineering for owner Gordon Rushton and then based on the Ffestiniog Railway. In July 1996 it was moved to South Wales, becoming the second working steam locomotive to be based on the Teifi Valley Railway, joining Hunslet 0-4-0ST *Alan George* — which at the time of this photograph was out of use and in the shed seen behind *Sgt Murphy*. *Geoff Lumb*

Left: Built by the Avonside Engine Co, Bristol, in 1933 for the Durham County Water Board's Burnhope Reservoir project, *Marchlyn* was delivered to Penrhyn in 1936. It was photographed on 25 August 1964 and is now in the USA. *Roger West*

17

Left: Built in 1885, *Winifred* was a member of Penrhyn's 'Port' class. With *Nesta*, built in 1899, it was one of the last Hunslets to work in the quarry. Sold in working order for £400, *Winifred* was one of six Penrhyn locos shipped to the USA in 1965. *Geoff Lumb*

Above: Glyder is an 0-4-0WT built by Barclay for the Durham County Water Board's Burnhope Reservoir project in 1931, arriving at Penrhyn in 1938. It was the last of the second-hand steam locomotives acquired, the last overhauled at Coed-y-Parc and, in 1962, reported to have been the last in service in the quarry. When photographed in September 1960 *Glyder* had apparently acquired a match truck. It was a member of the 1965 shipment to the USA. *Geoff Lumb*

Above: Cegin was another Barclay obtained from Durham, this time in 1936. On 25 August 1964 it was caught shunting the third quarry level. Within a year it was shipped to the USA, where it was last reported to be in Georgia. Use of the quarry railways ceased in 1965, although the quarry remains in production. *Roger West*

Fairbourne Railway

Above: First built as a 2ft gauge horse tramway designed to carry builders' materials during the development of Fairbourne in the late 19th century, the line remained in use and was extended to terminate at Barmouth Ferry, on the opposite bank of the Mawddach Estuary to Barmouth itself. Closed in 1915, the line was taken over the following year and converted to 15in gauge; at this point the use of steam locomotives commenced. Closed and damaged during World War 2, the line changed hands and was totally rebuilt before being reopened in 1947. Following a further change of ownership in 1984, a decision was taken to convert the line to 12¼in gauge, a move which was implemented during the winter of 1985/6. In August 1966, one of the Fairbourne Railway's 2-4-2s, *Siân*, receives attention to its fire while running along Penrhyn Drive North.
C.M. Whitehouse

Left: In the 1950s the Fairbourne Railway had some distinctive internal combustion locomotives. *Whippit Quick*, seen here on 13 September 1959, was built by Lister for the line in 1935 and rebuilt in the form shown in 1955. As the train approaches the Ferry terminus, Fairbourne village is seen behind. *P.B. Whitehouse/ C.M. Whitehouse Collection*

Above: 4-6-2 *Ernest W. Twining* was built in 1950 for the Dudley Zoo Railway, arriving at Fairbourne in 1961. Captured while running round at the Ferry, the houses of Fairbourne are seen behind. *Ernest W. Twining* left Fairbourne in 1984 and now runs in Japan. *C.M. Whitehouse Collection*

Left: On 1 September 1954 the Fairbourne Railway's Bassett-Lowke 4-4-2 *Count Louis* stands at the Ferry terminus with the canteen vehicle in the siding behind. The building of *Count Louis* was started in 1914 and finished in 1924, and it arrived at Fairbourne the following year, the last loco built by Bassett-Lowke. *P.B. Whitehouse/C.M. Whitehouse Collection*

Left: With the flag flying to indicate operation of train and ferry, *Dingo* is seen at the Ferry on 13 September 1959. Acquired by the railway in 1952, the stylish body, designed by the noted modeller and historian Ray Tustin, was fitted in 1954. *P.B. Whitehouse/ C.M. Whitehouse Collection*

Right: Guest 2-4-2 *Siân* at Penrhyn Point on a clear day, with the mountains of the Lleyn Peninsula visible in the distance. *C.M. Whitehouse Collection*

Festiniog Railway

Above: Opened in 1836 as a gravity-worked line carrying slate from quarries at Blaenau Ffestiniog to the harbour at Portmadoc, the Festiniog Railway converted to steam in 1863. Despite being successful in the second half of the 19th century, the railway went into decline in the 20th, closing in 1946. After protracted negotiations, reopening commenced from Portmadoc in 1955, Blaenau Ffestiniog being regained, after construction of a 2½-mile deviation route between Dduallt and Tanygrisiau, in 1982. In the period under review, original FR locos England 0-4-0TT *Prince* and Fairlie 0-4-4-0Ts *Taliesin* and *Merddin Emrys* were joined by Hunslet 0-4-0STs

Linda and *Blanche* from the Penrhyn Quarry Railway and the World War 1 Alco 2-6-2PT which was named *Mountaineer* on the FR. Here *Prince* and *Taliesin* stand at Harbour station in 1957; the Fairlie to take the advertised service train and *Prince* the extra 'flea' of four-wheeled stock. *P.B. Whitehouse/C.M. Whitehouse Collection*

Right: In 1960 *Prince* leaves Portmadoc (now Porthmadog) with a train of five bogies. The green and ivory carriage livery is still fondly recalled by many FR supporters. *Geoff Lumb*

Above: On 5 April 1969 *Earl of Merioneth*, previously *Livingston Thompson* and *Taliesin*, wheezes at the joints as it shunts a train of stock bearing the short-lived varnished teak livery. *C.M. Whitehouse*

Right: The World War 1 Alco 2-6-2PT *Mountaineer* carrying the original (1864) *Mountaineer's* bell in 1968, the year after the loco was donated to the FR by John Ransom. In the train are four of the wooden-bodied coaches built at Boston Lodge since 1964, one of which was new to traffic in 1968. *C.M. Whitehouse*

Left: The trident signal was a well-known feature of the Cob for over 40 years, until, weakened by rot, it was blown down during a gale in 1967. *Linda* passes by in 1963. *Millbrook House*

Right: At Minffordd in 1966, *Prince* passes with a works train. The station, an interchange for the Cambrian Coast line, was reopened 10 years earlier. *Geoff Lumb*

Left: Locomotives at Tan-y-bwlch water tower are still a centre of attraction, just as *Prince* was in September 1958. *J.C. Flemons/C.M. Whitehouse Collection*

Above: Gwyndy Bank, between Minffordd and Penrhyn, is a popular photographic location, shown in this photograph of a *Linda*-hauled train in 1962. The train has a quarrymen's carriage, noted for its very primitive seating, next to the locomotive.
C.M. Whitehouse

Above: Penrhyn was reopened in 1957. By using the headshunt there was just enough room for trains to cross here, the loop remaining in use until the 1970s. At that time the station was converted to become a volunteers' hostel. *Geoff Lumb*

Left: Prince heads towards Minffordd and Portmadoc along Gwyndy Bank, one of the Festiniog's distinctive drystone embankments, in the 1960s. *Millbrook House*

Right: In 1963 the FR launched its first advertised named train, 'Y Cymro' ('The Welshman'). It was the 3pm non-stop to Tan-y-bwlch, and is seen here crossing the Cei Mawr embankment. *Millbrook House*

Right: In September 1958, at the end of Tan-y-bwlch's first season as terminus, *Prince* waits to return to Portmadoc. Stationmistress Bessie Jones had resumed her prewar practice of serving refreshments from the station house, as indicated by the sign above the door. *C.M. Whitehouse Collection*

*Above:*Tan-y-bwlch was the FR's terminus for 10 years from 1958. Whilst the sidings are still grass covered and the running lines unfenced *Earl of Merioneth*, *Taliesin* until 1961, sets off for Portmadoc. *C.M. Whitehouse Collection*

Above: Fairlie *Merddin Emrys* returned to service in 1961 and is seen leaving Tan-y-bwlch during that year. The running lines have been cleared of grass but the siding remains buried. *Millbrook House*

Above: Blanche, by now in what has become recognised as typical Festiniog condition, with tender cab, is ignored by both fireman and ice-cream-eating child while waiting for the road. *C.M. Whitehouse*

Right: After a 10-year period of consolidation, the line between Tan-y-bwlch and Dduallt was reopened in 1968. From a vantage point no longer available due to tree growth, *Linda* is seen leaving Tan-y-bwlch for Dduallt in that year. *C.M. Whitehouse*

Vale of Rheidol Railway

Above: The Vale of Rheidol Railway was opened in 1902 to carry ore from the Rheidol Valley to Aberystwyth, and passengers to the ever-popular Devil's Bridge. Later operated by the Cambrian Railways, Great Western Railway and British Railways, it became, in 1988, the last steam railway operated by British Rail and, in 1989, the first railway sold by it complete with motive power and rolling stock. At 12 miles long the 2ft gauge line is notable for the continuous 1 in 50 gradient between Aberffrwd and Devil's Bridge. On 15 September 1955 the 1.45pm (left) and 2.30pm trains wait to leave Aberystwyth's narrow gauge station, the roofs of the standard gauge station being seen behind them; the locos are Nos 8 and 9. 1955 was the last year of the red and cream carriage livery. After the 1967 season Vale of Rheidol trains operated from the former Carmarthen line bay in the main line station. *P.B. Whitehouse/C.M. Whitehouse Collection*

Above: On a busy day No 9 crosses the timber Rheidol river bridge. Unusually, the train stretches to seven bogies and a four-wheeled van; in the 1988 sale document the British Railways Board claimed that the maximum load was six cars carrying 300 passengers. The Great Western carriage livery was applied in 1956.
Millbrook House

Above: A more typical formation is seen in this view, where the line runs parallel to the river as it approaches Capel Bangor. The picture shows how tidy the trackside used to be kept. *C.M. Whitehouse Collection*

Right: In 1964 the Rheidol carriages were painted Cambrian green with yellow lettering. No 9 is seen pounding up the grade towards Nantyronen. *P.B. Whitehouse/C.M. Whitehouse Collection*

Above: On 15 August 1964 No 7 *Owain Glyndwr* takes water at Aberffrwd, the location of the last operational passing loop on the line. *Geoff Lumb*

Right: A classic Rheidol scene, with the train high above the river, approaching Rheidol Falls Halt, and the famous 'Rheidol stag', the result of tipping lead mine spoil, on the opposite side of the valley. No 9 was caught on 2 August 1955. *T.B. Owen/C.M. Whitehouse Collection*

Left: 2-6-2T No 9 *Prince of Wales* nears Llanbadarn as it rolls back to Aberystwyth. Built at Swindon in 1924, No 9 was named in 1956. *C.M. Whitehouse Collection*

Right: No 8 *Llewelyn* passes the Erwtomau mine site, one of many former lead mines which riddle the area on both sides of the valley. *C.M. Whitehouse*

Right: At Devil's Bridge on 15 September 1955, No 8 waits to return to Aberystwyth with the 4.14pm departure. The following year the locomotives received their names. *P.B. Whitehouse/ C.M. Whitehouse Collection*

Talyllyn Railway

Above: The Talyllyn Railway was opened in 1865, designed to serve the Bryn Eglwys slate quarry, near its terminus at Abergynolwyn. Against all the odds it was to survive, relying only on its original two steam locomotives, five four-wheel carriages and a diminishing number of its 50-odd wagons, to become, in 1951, the first railway run with volunteer support. Three additions were quickly made to the railway's steam locomotive fleet: two from the Corris Railway, via British Railways, in 1951, and a Barclay 0-4-0WT in 1954. The Railway celebrated its centenary in 1965. According to *Talyllyn News*, 'The Centenarian' was supposed to be the 13.10 departure from Wharf between 24 May and 2 July, comprising original TR stock; however, its inaugural run was on 1 June and the photographer recorded taking this photograph in September, when stock included the Abergynolwyn refreshment van and the restored Corris Railway coach! The occasion might have been the Society's AGM day. *P.B. Whitehouse/C.M. Whitehouse Collection*

Above: 0-4-0WT No 2 *Dolgoch* was badly run-down in 1951 and only kept going with difficulty. The load was shared with other locos in 1952, and in 1953 *Dolgoch* became spare engine. The locomotive was sent away for overhaul between 1954 and 1963. It is seen newly restored at Pendre on 14 September 1963.
Ken Cooper/C.M. Whitehouse Collection

Left: Locomotive No 1 0-4-2ST *Talyllyn* was worn out when the Talyllyn Railway Preservation Society commenced operations; on 24 March 1957 it was pulled down to Wharf station for transportation to Brierley Hill for rebuilding. *P.B. Whitehouse/ C.M. Whitehouse Collection*

Right: A locomotive taking water at Dolgoch is always popular with photographers, as seen in this view of No 1 *Talyllyn* at the old water tower. In 1961 a new water tower was located further east to allow longer trains to stand in the platform. *C.M. Whitehouse Collection*

Right: On 14 June 1958 *Talyllyn* was photographed, rebuild completed, in Gibbons Bros Ltd yard before being loaded up for return to Towyn. *C.M. Whitehouse Collection*

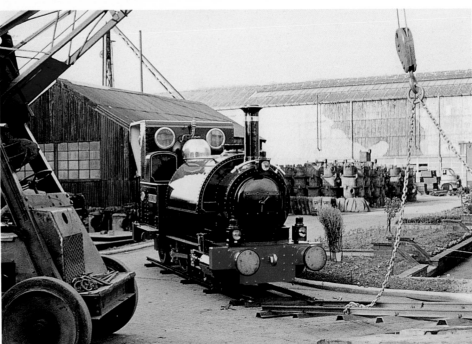

Left: A portrait of No 1 *Talyllyn* running round its train, an evening excursion, at Brynglas.
P.B. Whitehouse/C.M. Whitehouse

Right: Catching the sun and making a splendid sight, the veteran *Talyllyn* runs over the Dolgoch viaduct in 1961. *C.M. Whitehouse*

Above: Corris Railway 0-4-2ST No 3 was built by Hughes in 1878. Following the closure of the Corris Railway in 1948, No 3 was stored at Machynlleth until purchased, for £25 plus carriage to Towyn, by the TR in 1951. Narrow wheel treads caused problems on the TR's shaky track but its use did take the pressure off No 2. A notable feature at this time was its operation facing downhill, to ease crew access to the cab, the vacuum brake cylinder blocking the other side. At Abergynolwyn on a fine afternoon the photographer's wife and daughter pass the time with the loco crew. *P.B. Whitehouse/C.M. Whitehouse Collection*

Right: In June 1957 No 3 was captured shunting works stock at Rhydyronen. The siding was removed in 1974. *J.C. Flemons/C.M. Whitehouse Collection*

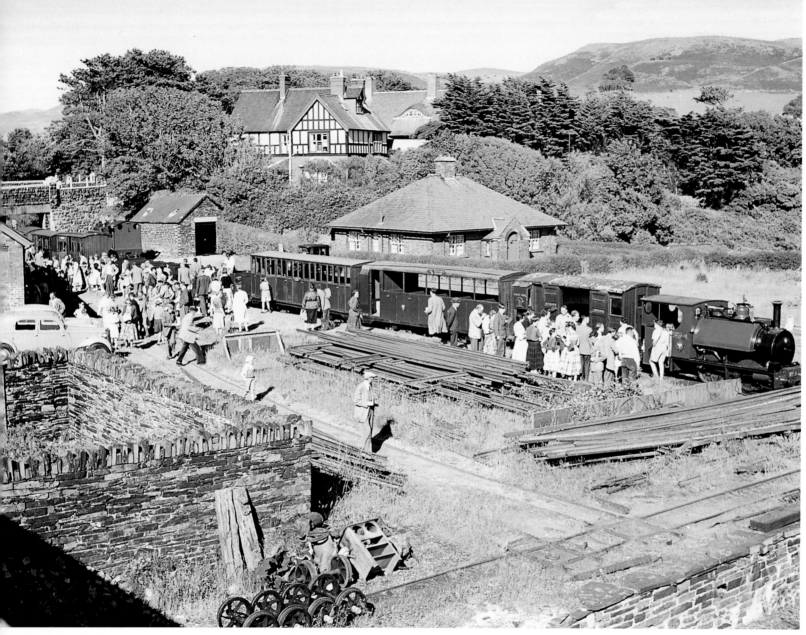

Left: Passengers cluster round No 3 at Wharf station in 1957. The picture shows the station layout almost unaltered since pre-preservation days; the yard on the left is now the site of the Narrow Gauge Railway Museum. Behind the train is *Russell*, displayed at Towyn for 10 years from 1955 and now a star attraction on the Welsh Highland Railway. The varied stock in the train is worthy of examination.
Millbrook House

Above: Ex-Corris Railway 0-4-2ST No 4 was named *Edward Thomas*, after the TR's pre-preservation manager. It was out of order when purchased in 1951 and was overhauled free of charge by Hunslet, successor to Kerr, Stewart which built No 4 in 1921. The overhaul was completed in time for the loco to enter TR service in 1952. Early pictures of No 4 are distinguished by the absence of running plates.
J.C. Flemons/C.M. Whitehouse Collection

Above: However, by June 1957, following an overhaul of No 4's motion, running
plates were fitted. *J.C. Flemons/C.M. Whitehouse Collection*

Above: In 1958 No 4 emerged from Pendre Works equipped with a Giesl ejector,
which it retained until 1969. The photograph was taken on 27 May 1958.
Ken Cooper/C.M. Whitehouse Collection

Right: The Talyllyn Railway obtained Barclay 0-4-0WT No 6 *Douglas* following an appeal to industry for surplus equipment in 1952. Donated by Abelson & Co (Engineers) Ltd and named after that company's managing director, No 6 arrived at Towyn in 1954. Dai and Herbert Jones are seen on the footplate on 23 September 1955. *J.C. Flemons/ C.M. Whitehouse Collection*

Left: It will be seen that both the position of the plates... *P.B. Whitehouse/C.M. Whitehouse Collection*

Right: ...and the colour scheme had changed by 26 September 1958. *J.C. Flemons/C.M. Whitehouse Collection*

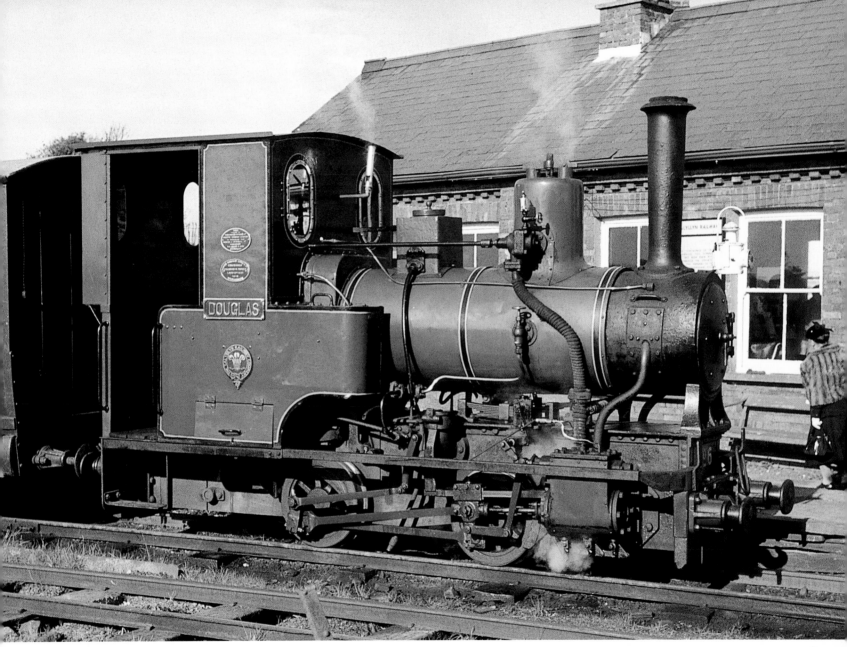

Welshpool & Llanfair Light Railway

Left: The Welshpool & Llanfair Light Railway was opened in 1903 to serve a dispersed agricultural community. Operated first by the Cambrian Railways and after the 1923 Grouping by the Great Western Railway, the 2ft 6in gauge line lasted until 1956 in British Railways management. Passenger services had been withdrawn in 1931, the line surviving on a traffic substantially of coal and lime westwards to Llanfair Caereinion and sheep and cattle back to Welshpool market. In 1955 No 822, one of the line's two Beyer Peacock 0-6-0s, stands outside Welshpool loco shed before setting off through the town and onwards to Llanfair with the daily goods.
C.M. Whitehouse Collection

Above: No 822 was originally and is now again named *The Earl*. By 1955 the nameplates had been removed to protect them from souvenir hunters.
C.M. Whitehouse Collection

Above: The daily goods at Castle Caereinion. The village that the station was intended to serve is off to the right of the picture, well out of sight. Several W&L stations had loops but only that at Castle Caereinion was signalled for passing trains before preservation, and that was out of use by the 1930s. The other loop lines were used as double-ended sidings.
C.M. Whitehouse Collection

Above: Reopened by the preservation company in 1963, the centre of operations transferred to Llanfair Caereinion, nine miles away, as no official support could be obtained for retaining the section between the Welshpool terminus, close to the town's standard gauge station, and Raven Square, on the town's western edge. However, the track remained *in situ* for a short time and several works and members' trains were operated over the town section. On 6 April 1963, 60 years after the line's opening, *The Earl* waits to leave Welshpool with the official reopening train. The carriages were obtained from the Admiralty's Lodge Hill & Upnor Railway. *C.M. Whitehouse Collection*

Above: The largest structure on the line is the handsome six-arch Brynelyn Viaduct, near Cyfronydd, pictured with a works train, including passenger vehicles, passing over it on 26 March 1964. *P.B. Whitehouse/C.M. Whitehouse Collection*

Right: The Banwy Bridge, the railway's other notable structure, was almost the preservation company's downfall when, in December 1964, the pier seen here being crossed by *The Countess* and its train was undermined by flood waters during a severe storm; fortunately, the Army came to the rescue and rebuilt it as a training exercise, the line reopening in August 1965. *C.M. Whitehouse Collection*

Left: The Earl arrives at Llanfair Caereinion, passing the home signal, on 22 July 1970. The train consists of the Austrian coaches obtained in 1968. These were the first of a number of items, both coaches and locomotives, obtained from overseas, which continue to give the railway the distinctive appearance that endears it to both enthusiast and visitor alike.
C.M. Whitehouse

Snowdon Mountain Railway

Above: Opened in 1896, the Snowdon Mountain Railway is a 700mm gauge line built to use the Swiss Dr Roman Abt's rack system. The 4½-mile journey from Llanberis takes an hour, the trains rising from 353ft to 3,493ft above sea level. Ascending the mountain all trains are propelled, as seen in this view of No 8 *Eryri* crossing the Afon Hwch at Llanberis; the railway's depot is on the right of the picture and Llanberis village is behind the train. At this point the gradient changes from 1 in 50 to 1 in 6. *P.B. Whitehouse/C.M. Whitehouse Collection*

Left: The Afon Hwch viaduct is 500ft long, the track gradient 1 in 8½, the largest structure on the line. Grazing sheep ignore No 8 *Eryri* as it returns to Llanberis. *C.M. Whitehouse*

Above: No 8 *Eryri* was built in 1923, the last steam locomotive built new for the line. The chocolate brown carriage livery was used for a period in the late 1950s. *Millbrook House*

Left: On 31 July 1965 a train is seen approaching Halfway; the photographer's vantage point is above the deepest (20ft) cutting on the line. *Geoff Lumb*

Above: Every operating day a train takes staff, supplies and water to the Summit; No 3 *Wyddfa* is seen on this duty in the early 1960s. *Geoff Lumb*

Left: The Snowdon locos were built to two basic designs, in 1895/6 and 1922/3, the latter batch having shorter side tanks, although of greater capacity. One of the later engines, No 8 *Eryri*, approaches Clogwyn, with the tips of the Dinorwic quarries behind, on 19 April 1963. *Ken Cooper/C.M. Whitehouse Collection*

Above: The track gang has prepared for renewal and the adjacent footpath is well worn by the feet of thousands of walkers; No 4 *Snowdon* approaches Clogwyn on the return journey to Llanberis on 9 June 1965. *Ken Cooper/C.M. Whitehouse Collection*

Above: One of the older locos nears the Summit in 1965, the distant panorama of Llyn Padarn and the Caernarfonshire plains stretching towards the Menai Strait beyond. *Geoff Lumb*

Right: On 9 June 1965 No 5 *Moel Siabod* climbs from Clogwyn towards the Summit visible though still a long way off. *Ken Cooper/ C.M. Whitehouse Collection*

Left: A classic portrait of a Snowdon locomotive, as seen on 24 August 1961 — No 5 *Moel Siabod*, built in 1896, at Clogwyn, high above the Llanberis Pass in the distance. The driver has installed a 'draught excluder' in the cab doorway.
Ken Cooper/C.M. Whitehouse Collection

Above: No 6 *Padarn's* driver appears to be at prayer while standing at Clogwyn in the 1950s. Built in 1922, No 6 was then named *Sir Harmood*.
C.M. Whitehouse Collection